VELOCI

2006 Agnes Lynch Starrett Prize

PITT POETRY SERIES
Ed Ochester, Editor

Velocity

Nancy Krygowski

UNIVERSITY OF
PITTSBURGH PRESS

Published by the University of Pittsburgh Press, Pittsburgh, Pa., 15260
Copyright © 2007, Nancy Krygowski
Manufactured in the United States of America
Printed on acid-free paper
10 9 8 7 6 5 4 3 2 1
ISBN 13: 978-0-8229-5977-9
ISBN 10: 0-8229-5977-1

CONTENTS

Velocity

THIS LOSS, ANY:

holds on: tree branch thin: signs dark doors: inhabits the dark spaces
on the checkerboard floor: dried cornflake the sponge missed: fingers that tug
a child's stuck zipper: clutch broken glass. A living thing, loss has two ears:
one roves left: right: the other goes inside: listens
to the names: Elias: Annette: Grace: teeth against teeth: stop it: begin
again:
this loss, any: wears a body: pearls a neck: yellow caution tape slapping
in wind: plastic pink flowers frozen in ground: untamable as smell: names
on marble that won't move lips: its own and only sister: a too-tight
dress. This loss, any, walks the highway's grit: Coke bottle filled
with a teenager's piss: shallow brown river and then the flood: hands
tossing sandbags: sandbags: the makeshift: the taming:
the wall:

1

SUITCASE OF MY LIFE

People gathered *not family, strangers?*
in our poorly lit kitchen
to eat jellied pigs' feet everyday. *seems like a bold statement*
Or so it seemed. *retracts previous statement*
In my young girl's mind
those days strung together
to make an eternity of strange death
in the center of which
was the table, the beige bowl, ⎤ *these lines work well to bring the*
the clear gelatin,   ⎬ *image into focus by getting*
the hooves.   ⎦ *shorter & shorter.*

I had a theory for life in general:
All my faked yawns made me *why fake a yawn? pretending to*
a wide open space of air   *be bored? tired?*
without a purpose. Almost
invisible, I was a city   *what exactly is her theory?*
without lights.

My name is Nancy.
My mom's is Anne.
My grandmothers' are
Anastasia and Antoinette.
I have a sister, Annette.
When we lived together
you could hear sighs
from one room to another.
First her, then her, her,
her, then me. *last because that's how it alway is? or oney*
            sighs b/c everyone else sighs?
There were the yellow-eyed birds
who refused to tell the future
that itched at our hands.

↑ the future itched @ their hands?

[left margin annotations:]

a family member has died and people come over to visit? am I bringing too much personal experience to this poem & .: not reading accurately?

almost too much here. I kind of want the 1st line to come after the other names (or would that be too conspicuous?)

what is this about?

5

Birds?
family? [They] knew I was destined
to be a silent egg, cracked open,
accidentally, past my prime. *interesting*

[They] knew the big, fat cow
we never named, never loved
would outlive us all.

mortality? the cow = important
b/c it = unimportant?

important that = "They knew" rather than "we"

6

THE BUS COMES, THE GIRL GETS ON

The famous linguist Walter Ong
says to subordinate—
because, if, since—

is a sign of a literate
culture, and I think I know
what he means:

Since the sun didn't rise today,
night walked on
in its thick black shoes.
Or,
If night walks on
in its thick black shoes,
there will be no bus,
there is no girl.

See what I can do?
Take the things of the world
and put them in an orderly order:

Since the sun rises, the birds sing.

And,
If the birds sing, the sun will rise,
the bus will come.

And,
Because the crows are angry,
yelling in their man-of-the-house way,
the sun rises,
a rifle
in her delicate hands,
crosshairs curtaining
her one good eye.

Like every morning.

Walter Ong talks sentences—
and though he loves how,
in the morning, light becomes pink
as his imaginary wife's slippers,
as swirling and red as the grenadine
in last night's drink,

and though he would never cage
a bird,
I wonder if even he sometimes forgets
the trickiness in deciding
who or what

gets control,
and
the complex beauty
of and and and.

HOW SHE LEARNED TO LISTEN

When the father's car pulls into the drive (it was green, he used chewed
Juicy Fruit and Bondo to cover the rust), she slips off to hide

in the closet, the one used to hang coats still cold from the outside air.
(The muffler was bad, an unplaced rattle rattled his nerves.)

She slides behind wool, long and black, behind the brothers'
hooded sweatshirts, the smell of burning leaves. She slips

like air that swallows sound, lets it go, steers clear of her own
flowered slicker, afraid its lightness will tip off a sequence of sorry

clinks, empty hangers that clang like the sideways U of the fence gate
as a hand shoves it up (and the gate swings open and a boy walks in). She stands

like a lamp, like a ketchup bottle, like two trees on a windless day.
She stands like a bookcase, a refrigerator, like a broken leg. She stands until

the father opens the closet door, head turned, arm reaching like a blindfolded kid
with a stick, a piñata. She sticks her arms out, yells *surprise!* (as if it really were)

in her high coat-muddled voice. He goes along with this, mouth puckered
in a small O. (A tunnel. *This is where I came from*, she thinks.)

Sometime later, she can sit in a room full of people, hear behind their voices
the secret of a heater turning on, the soon-to-be clank of air trapped in pipes.

VELOCITY

I was riding my bike
     on a road in Georgia. Weeds
          and ditches, trees, me and solitude,

the heat. I was 16, in love
     with speed, long hair trailing behind
          like a visible wind.

I was happy. I was 16.
     Then two men in a truck.
          We all know what wind means:

Free. Two men and me.
     The sun was sinking. I was 16.
          The one in the passenger seat

reached out to grab
     the wind. No use
          describing the jerk of

my head, the scream.
     I was 16. I lived.
          No use describing the force

of a hand linked to a truck,
     two drinking men, what
          "back roads Georgia" means.

All of us were traveling, near equal
     velocity, back when I still loved danger,
          speed. Downhill. Back

when I understood "free."
     If this were a math problem,
          it would read, *A girl*

on a bike travels at 20 mph.
　　Two men in a truck
　　　moving at a slightly faster speed

pull up. One grabs her hair.
　　What will the outcome be?
　　　I was 16. Innocent enough to love

solitude, danger, speed.
　　On a rural road in Georgia,
　　　I liked to be hot and fast and

free. A bike the color
　　of the sun. I was happy
　　　as a peach. The man tugged

at the wind. And then the crumple
　　that was me, the gravel
　　　pitting my pure heat. I was 16,

had been learning, slowly,
　　to love my solitude, a fire
　　　inside. And then, so suddenly,

the wind in his hands,
　　bloody and brown, the holes
　　　in my skin. The force of a knowledge

dark as speed, hard
　　as free. The answer: I
　　　lived. I was 16.

SHE DIES:

Watery

breath

watery breath watery

watery sky and bird breath

a brother

(the engineer)

looks

at his

watch:

5:23

:my hand

from

her

hand

I unhook

the earrings

from

what were

her ears

NIGHT EATS THE LAST OF IT

My dead sister's daughter calls to tell me
about her first kiss. Annette's bones

lay in ground an hour away from me,
fourteen hours from her daughter.

We can't talk to them. I forget which clothes
we buried her in—it didn't matter.

Bones never talk back.
I remember her cigarettes, arriving

at her house as one started a small fire
while she slept from sadness on the couch.

Or the ones she said she loved
and dropped, slack fingered, onto her death-

bed when the morphine kicked lovingly in.
Cigarettes didn't matter then. Annette didn't

love roses. Today, a boy gave her kissed
daughter six; she calls to ask how to save them.

Which means she's asking how to kill,
how to force them to lose what she loves—

the pure red color, the velvet, the cloying, beautiful smell.
There are many kinds of people in the world,

but there are only two kinds of people in the world:
those who've helped a person die

and those who haven't. A book I'm reading tells
about a daughter who "still measures events

on a child's scale of fair and unfair." I hang
a rose upside down from Annette's picture on the wall.

This isn't fair. When I see her daughter, I'll light
a cigarette, watch as her lips breathe a pure burning kiss.

STILL WET

Friday the thirteenth. I am superstitious, and my friend just told me she fucked a man without protection, without that extra, squeaky bland wall between their skin. She said, *He didn't come inside me,* and *Isn't sex always the mystery?* and wants to know what I think. Sometimes I don't know if I can be honest, I forget what honest is. She is getting married to another man, one who likes the sad seed of a heart she keeps tucked in her chest like a pair of old black panties. When *they* fuck, she says, she thinks about wind and the spaces between leaves. She wants to know what I think. Sometimes I don't like the man who has sex with me. Sometimes I pull his bones into mine like they are breath, sometimes I hate the barrier that is our skin. When I was in love, I needed to squeeze and bite and hit. I think I loved a man on his knees, my finger up his ass, the power in me, whatever that means. The bony woman at the corner store is suspicious of me, how I show up once a week in this neighborhood, buy orange juice, a newspaper, maybe milk. Here, everyone is somebody, so who can I be? This time it is way past morning, and my hair is still wet. I am freshly washed, freshly fucked, and missing the ache that has lingered from the end of my last love. There is an equation here—

(sex minus love) (love plus pain) (if sex or love, then _____)

—I can't figure it out. The woman's overly wrinkled, tanned skin folds up as she greets me, but her blue eyes stay hard and thick. She asks how I am. I am not supposed to be honest, but I can't remember how to lie. I think about my friend. She's wondering about pre-ejaculatory fluid and wants to know what I think. I press toward the woman a palm full of change. Our skins touch as I pour the metal from my hand to hers, exact amount, an equal exchange.

THE NEXT TIME I WAS ROBBED

was with a knife: wide and long,
rounded dull, the kind for frosting

a cake's slumped middle. The way
a wrist makes a swirl

is how the man made his way
toward me. How little

I knew. Lump, then face,
then hint of a point.

The man and knife
covered in a blanket:

This is what emptiness smells like:

Motel curtains. Summer dirt kicked up
by the car that never comes back.

I said, *Henry, this man wants to rob me.*

Soft as a cake's belly, the dull yellow
a second before the toothpick goes in,

I'd never really *wanted,*
I couldn't know the pointed

shame of a woman who so wants
love, she's taken for money.

I was like a small town high school boy
who dreams only of joining the army.

I said again, *Henry, he wants to rob me.*

A blanket wants to be warmed,
wants to be the one who sleeps.

A knife wants to be a fork,
wants to be the one who eats.

The man said: *Bitch,*
give me the money.

IT'S A GOOD DAY

when, at the Shop-and-Save's express line,
I am flanked by two middle-aged men,
the first of whom hands
the fountain-haired checkout girl
a big tub of Vaseline—
his only purchase, no wedding ring,
no Pampers, no Ace bandages,
just Vaseline,
and he doesn't meet her eyes,
and she doesn't meet his.
As he moves toward the sliding doors,
his entire body swings.
Then me—milk, frozen whole okra,
a roll of transparent tape—I wonder:
is someone trying to make sense of *this?*
I look for pennies in the bottom of my purse
and look, too, at the word, *pennies,*
which could almost be the other word,

because of Mr. Vaseline and the happy thing
he is off to do, and because I loved a man
with a beautiful penis, one whose hand,
right now, probably grips a pencil
with the faith of a mathematician who accepts
there are no perfect circles in the world,
that *perfect circle* exists
not in the smooth-edged copper I slip
into the cashier's hand,

not in the three-pack of Trojans
the man behind me tosses down
on the still-moving conveyor belt,
but only *in theory*.
He sticks out three one-dollar bills exactly
as the girl hands me the same.
So I smile.
At the mystery of synchronicity,
at the man's beautiful impatience,
at the fact that I, too, had a lover,
one whose tobacco-colored eyes stared
at numbers, triangles, letters
that stood for numbers,
and wondered if a mathematical proposition
could be proven by appealing to experience,
as if a perfect, deep kiss could be proof
of the imperfect circle
of long, consistent love.
The answer, I am told, is *no*.
But now I remember, happily,
exactly what I mourn.

SHE DIED

and she had a daughter but she had a daughter and I fed her
mashed potatoes but I fed her mashed potatoes and picked out
the clothes we buried her in so she died and I lit a cigarette but
she said she would walk again and she died and I took the empty
bedpan but she died and I ate the peppers she had canned and she
died and her daughter was kissed and she died but we sang songs
full of morphine and Percodan so she died yet she died and she died.

PRESENT

The future is fear and the past is regret . . .
Allegra says, giving advice. But in the silent

ellipses that complete her thought, I miss the point,
forget here, now, the woman in front of me with butterfly

eyes, the waiter's accent that tongues my ears, the simple
pleasure in the bell's ring as another friend comes in.

I'm afraid of regret, I say, *so I guess*
I choose fear, and start to prepare

for a life of shallow-breathed days, a heart that pounds
to escape. Once before, I wrote a poem called "Present,"

which was about both uses of that word.
Except the gift was a glimpse into Alzheimer's eyes—

each time you see a leaf you ask, *What's that? That? That?*—
and the moment was a bald Christmas tree washing up on a beach.

The dinner with friends started and ended and my life
was changed. On Wednesday, I kept my distance

from strangers and their sneakily smiling dogs. On Thursday,
my conversation with the landlord, who, on Monday,

I was sure I loved, was short. I watched the whereabouts
of his ninety-year-old hands. On Friday, Allegra corrected me.

That saying—it's about living in the present. But my head
was locked in a talk I planned to have with Linn,

who'd been debating *pills vs. asphyxiation* and who's peaceful
now that she's decided how she'd like to die.

2

DEAR BRAIN,

dear student of disaster,
heart's manipulative sister,
I'm tired. Happy New Year.
This time, you'll be a road sign
with an arrow. The sign's metal pole.
A bicycle tire's rim—
no, too important, too thin.
Rear wheel on a front-wheel drive car.
Hill in the distance,
shoes in a box. It's those
late-night shopping sprees, your constant
chirping. Memory mongering.
Slow down. I've got some
feeling to do. You'll be
the just-in-case, only-if-necessary
underwear in the bottom drawer.

Sweet brain,
needy brain,

thank you for your fires, misfires,
synapses, and trials. I like your
college campus, white equations floating
on blue green seas. But I get lost
in the late afternoon composition
class no one knows exists.
I love your tuned guitar strings,
hard bass beat. I'm tired of your sheep
that need shearing to make a sweater
with a hole in the elbow
that will need patching.
Here. Have this sweater, more water
for your tea. Blue rocker in the corner.
Please, take this blank book to read.

I GET HAPPY WHEN I SHUDDER

at the truck full of cows
going off to slaughter. Cows
with shit caked onto black
fur—what happens to the fur?
(It swings as a purse
from a woman's clean hand.)
Cows that are still cow-happy
rubbing necks and noses
against corrugated truck walls, the holes
allowing for intricate scratching—
smooth here, plucky there—happy
I can still so easily feel

this sentimental—
imagining them imagining their babies
and how before their bodies got
so cow-edible big, they ran
on stick-girl legs.
(I imagine, too,
though I'm not sure why,
a college boy having sex
with a retarded girl
who is happy—
why shouldn't she be?—
as she tugs at her nipples, raises her hips,
bats big cow lashes, and doesn't see
the stretched-out underwear
stuck on her foot.)

A cowbell hangs on the back
of the truck. I make up
a story about how
it lulls these doomed to dreams
of when their mother's milk
was theirs alone.
This is pure lie, as is
my choice to ignore the pure beauty
of the dried-up bull scrotum—
a thick and wrinkled rose—
swaying soundless and guilty
beside the bell.

MORNING GLORIES

How did I know
the deep purple blue
climbing the playground
fence (I was barely 10)
would turn to black ball
seeds I could eat

eat until I lifted out
of my plaid skirt
life, a blouse the white
of no dreams?
How did I know?

I didn't know
the word *hallucinogenic*,
didn't want to know
I knew something bad
about the pills
in the bottom
of my sister's fringed purse.

Fourth grade, Catholic school
stomachaches,
poster on the schoolroom door.
A pretty older girl
tucked into simple cloth,

hung with a cross,
"Could YOU be a nun?"

Do I have to?

Did I have to learn
the guilt so well, the dry heave
of *I can do wrong?*

Not breathing
makes a stomach hurt.
Fear turns a heart
wafer thin. Not wanting

cuts a path not to good, but to the bad
stop of a white gloved hand,
wall of *No, no.*

How did I know
to want that blue ride away
from kickball, flash cards,
the kicked-in cold air
of incense dark
as the stations of the cross,

that I'd have to eat so many seeds
I might throw up?

Unfair. Each year,
Come watch how Christ died.

BOTTLE OF HATE, BOTTLE OF SUN

Black kids hunch
in men's bodies,
angle hips
and arms
out

as they talk
and stop
in the middle

of the car-fast street.

They count on drivers'
kindness
to keep them safe

as they court
small rage

then grace

in the hands of the white guy
who assumes they'll move

then swerves
hard left
to save them,

hard right
to save himself.

He doesn't yell. Drives home.
Glass of ice water, can of soup.

Some hates
quiet us, leave us

delicate and stiff
as a bird's curved beak.

I wanted to drown a boy
for calling me fat
as my sister was dying.

I was at the beach,
on a break from caretaking.
I walked away.

He's about twenty now.

I drown him
a lot in my head.

One of the street boys
carries a glass bottle
shiny as his dark
swerving eyes.

How can laughter
not be about happiness?

He raises it up,
catches the sun.

Bottle of hate, bottle of sun.
Bottle of our small
history.

Even the angel
who watches over

hate
is caught thinking

about *cause.* Thinking *mercy.*

The angel says,
Go ahead,

smash the glass
that will anger
the storekeepers,
puncture your bike tire,

cut your mother's
sweet, sandaled foot.

WHAT THE NEXT VOICE SAID:

Simple advice:
Take this with a grain of salt.
(Sweet potatoes, green
green spinach,

tomatoes pink with lies.
Salt pinched
between forefinger and thumb,
balanced, antigravity,

above carrots, onions, lentils bouncing
in a pot.
Salt thrown over a shoulder,
traveling to linoleum, a wish—

health, love, a new car—
on its back.
Thick utilitarian salt

leaves a history, raised and white,
on the black leather boots
that leave their own
damp history
inside my door.)

CONTROL

I pulled on the tight black slip, the already ripped
   hose, lipstick called *Blood*, told him how I'd leave
      the red of those lips on his beautiful dick. I told him—

Mike, I said—*imagine the tight circle they'll make.*
   I wanted to feel unburdened of the mind's hurts
      (he'd left me, vague note on the well-made bed;

came back; left me, he came back); I wanted
   only the body's imagination, only to control
      his pleasure of me. I pressed the lip of my wineglass

to the glass of his, then to his real lips, kept him
   at arm's length while I twisted his nipples, wiped
      the wet from between my legs across his neck, kissed,

licked. That's when he knocked me to the bed. I felt
   the stem slip out of my hand, saw the sheets stain, thought,
      What takes out red wine? This wasn't what I'd planned. He

pulled the hose's holes into bloodless cuts,
   stuck the short-nailed fingers of his other hand
      into my mouth, flipped my body around, shoved my shoulders

down, pulled up on my waist, pulled apart
   my resilient knees. My right cheek butted into the head-
      board's bars, divided into bone and lump of fat. *Ugly*, I thought,

my face must look so ugly. I loved him.
   I wanted him to love me, to not leave this small life
      I thought I understood, our little house. I told myself:

I like it from behind / I like the small pain /
   I like the stopping of time / the shoving of my ass /
      I like having to ask, Who is this man? Who is this man?

SHE DIED

after a burning cigarette the clothes we buried
her in since the clothes we buried her in her
daughter's first kiss because of small
spoonfuls of mashed potatoes, morphine,
unshaven legs, before the daughter was found
drunk in a boat with unsavory men because
the TV is always on anger the lie of *when I*
can walk again because the daughter's first
gynecological exam after shampooing the dead
hair on a dying head after the small shit
in a bedpan after no shit in the bedpan if she
had a daughter before the dog died while
singing songs filled with Percodan since eating
peppers she had canned because of one
missing breast   the clothes we buried her in.

ARM

One day on the bus I was playing with my sleeve, and I found it—a
hem. So I pulled at the big stitches and let one arm down. The coat
fit me perfectly then. I did the other arm too, except for three stitches
that wouldn't come undone. Too tight, probably the first to be put in.
I broke off the thread, left them. The woman with short arms before
me was practical, efficient. That was weeks ago, and I'd forgotten
about all this, at least most of the time. Other times I'd play with the
little lump of turned over material, the remnant of the hem. Today,
on the bus again, I didn't have much to think about, or maybe I did.
I felt the lump, decided to get rid of it. I took out my knife—did I
mention I had a knife? I pulled out the blade, then looked up. The
bus was starting to slow. This could be dangerous. I saw a woman,
brown eyes looking right at mine. She looked at my hands, and
she looked at the knife, and those eyes and her mouth that was set
perfectly straight said, *What are you doing? What are you doing?* And to tell
the truth, I didn't know.

NOTHING ELSE WILL WORK

My friend is breaking down in tears. She stands in an inappropriate
doorway, the Save-A-Lot, where grapes are on sale,

79 cents. And somehow I think the most appropriate
response is to kiss her, to careen the mileage of my breasts

against hers, slip the muscle of my silent tongue
between those wobbly lips, touch her

teeth. She is not my lover. Her mascara leaks
down the hump of her cheeks. Her chin,

which I've always thought of as strong, wants to shake off
her face, start a practical life as a dental hygienist.

I put my hands, my short inappropriate hands,
on her shoulders, send the inadequacy

of my face toward hers. My small vocabulary
of comfort convinces me nothing else

will work. Pamela with her tears and me with my
hands, this blind tongue, stand, feet shuffling around the secret

device that tips off the store's automatic doors. Which blinked
and twitched. Which opened and closed. Which started and stopped.

DEAR PANTIES,

When the healer told me
about the bad energy in black
and red, how could I not think
about my lonely vagina,
how its walls feel only
each other, like holding
my own hand?

And how,
for years, walking through
my walled-in days, I've favored
these bad-girl colors, so at least
I could whisper,
    These are really hot,
as my own hands slide them off.

Dear new panties,
I choose your flowers—
orange and yellow and pink—
two days in a row

to brighten the parts of my body
so mostly my own
as I careen through South Dakota,
as I sit now in Sioux Falls,
where I can't find falls,
where men walk by in sun-tight skin
and ignore my *excuse me*'s
for directions. I don't want
their fingers, but can I have their eyes?

Here, I wear this superstition—
flowers blooming between my legs—
because my questions are windy
and wide as a prairie:
    Why does fear wall in a heart?
    What happens when a body
    becomes invisible?

It's too simple to say a prairie
is simply empty, to say
there are no answers.
Here, a world of grass
holds down the soil, digs down
in stringy curves the height of me,
finds water.

WHAT MIGHT BE GALAXIES AT MY FEET

On the night's sidewalk
after a storm, streetlights gather
in puddles. It is
as if cement and water
could hold galaxies—
the large light a sun,
the smaller ones
planets, each with its
mythical name.
On one, a boy stares into the mirror,
wonders how one nostril
could be bigger than the other.
On the planet's other side,
a woman finds a letter, a lump,
exactly what she wishes
didn't exist.
Looking down at this sky,
for this still second,
my feet feel at home.
And then the sky above me breaks,
and the first small drops
of other might-be galaxies
blur all my worlds.

SINCE THE WORLD WENT BAD

I wonder if my Russian neighbors
who don't know English,
who pronounce my name with serious
mouths that can't feel the girlishness
of its vowels, know the universal signal

for choking—
hands around your own throat—

if something so cartoonish *can* be universal,
or if they imagine that gesture signals
a sore throat, a hard or scary day.

Ever since the world went bad,
I've known I could die stupidly,

from forgetting water and electricity
don't mix, from being too hungry
to slow down,
chew,
and then breathe.

In France, a law says in an emergency
a person must help,
it is illegal not to.

The seriousness
of age or cancer

is for people who trust the world,
who need time to puzzle out
its plotting betrayal, but

I'll go down

surrounded by two Russian women
in plaid skirts, flowered shirts,
thick beige stockings wrinkling sturdy legs:

Aida and Marina smiling
like when I've asked to borrow salt.
Salt, I say,
trying to make every letter heard,
Salt,
my shaking, empty hand pointed down.

Aida and Marina, smiling, helpful,

and me, breathless, unable to laugh

or say, *I can't believe this*

or

of course.

3

DEAR BLACK PEACH,

and dear fruit flies,
queens of the quick/slow
good-bye, what does it feel like
to be so
finite?

Do you realize
the white ceiling lines
of your painted sky
will shut down on this day
of perfection,
your 24-hour life,
become a final darker-than-you
night?

On Wednesdays a person's life
feels blandly
infinite—
it is always Wednesday and
it will be Wednesday again and
how many Wednesdays until. . . .

But this Wednesday,
yours,
dear little ones,
you are masters of sweet industry,
masters of sex and your small
important love for life/death.

The peach has died,
but at what moment,
I can't say.
I keep it
and let you live your day.
I will buy
but not eat.

EVERYTHING

This has something to do
with what your heart does
when you see a crow
walking on the road
toward another dead animal
whose tail moves in the wind,
brushes against blood and stones,
says, *See, I'm alive.*
Tell me I'm alive.

And you're driving the car
heading toward that crow
when you remember fingers drumming
one at a time against a table.
You realize that sound is not a clock.
Fingers pounding in the quietest way
are not a clock. They are not time.
Time is an attitude toward a crow.

Statues of saints, arms raised, guard a cemetery.
You think those arms ask you to come in.
You look at your hands,
the steering wheel's simple circle,
and forget about blood.
Because that is everything.
Looking up and going straight is everything.

THIS HARDLY MAKES SENSE

                             I hardly remember
the details of you—except once I dreamed
you brought me a cup of coffee made thick
with cream, and once I blushed because all day
in Maelstrom—the bookstore of couches,
bounced checks, Henry, and me—
I stared at Picasso's *Harlequin*,
a little emptiness in my chest,
then realized when you walked in,
I had spent the day staring
at a younger, painted you. I:

                             am over thirty, kind.
I've drunk the spoiled milk of tragedy
(death, death, death) enough to know
I simply want beauty, happiness,
and know it's not that hard to find—
See how that man helps the woman into her wheelchair?
How she topples, then doesn't?
See this single bougainvillea flower?
Do you hear that word,
bougainvillea,
how it loves your mouth? You:

                             see with the small, smart eyes
of bats, carry a kind of silence
like a door around you,
have three beating hearts in your chest,
will explain them, I guess,
if asked. I won't ask.

                             With you, I
think there is no need to describe
my breasts, how these hips
can be traced down from my waist,
how that trip is like fog that turns waves

into sound, the wind so strong
your home twelve blocks away
doesn't exist. It doesn't need to.

                I have trouble loving,
sometimes, what I love: public
transportation, a tea kettle's whistle,
the dark and how
it always comes. I am naive
(often by choice), have recurring dreams,
don't shave my underarms,
never studied economics.

                You appear like a star
(suddenly just there),
pull on the small holes in your T-shirt,
stuff the insides of your shoes
with other people's secrets,
don't know my name.
(It is Nancy.)

My thrifty landlord bought a new furnace
when I moved in. He didn't want me to be cold. *You are*
beautiful, he says. *I mean it,*
I am eighty-seven, I have no reason
to say that, except to say it.

                I know this hardly
makes sense. But I want to ask you this:
Can I know you more? Or know you less?

LOIS SENDS ME A HOROSCOPE, AND I MAP MY WAY

Slowly, slow
down. Count

the stars on the night's
black abacus.

Look. Look.
It's easy

to find love.
The moon hangs

like a soft grapefruit.
A stranger's to-do list

sticks to the ground,
buy chocolate,

its surprise.
Can a person wait

if she isn't sure
what she's waiting for?

An iris shoot hoards a guarantee
of serious purple, curious yellow.

One push of wind
leaves its handprint

on my neck, sways the hair
on my head, the loose tangle

of twigs hanging
from this one tree.

TIME ZONES

The kids next door have turned Red Rover
into a rap song—each syllable
a force of air, more-than-full
rest beat between *red*
and *roe,*
empty space
before the *ver.*

This morning,

I'm a math problem, I can go
anywhere.
One car, one woman, *x*
amount of time. The driving
minutes that make up
one day could have me two,
maybe three hours
earlier in life's red

tomorrow. The sun
is overhead at noon

no matter where you are. Time's
a song *(ten-fifteen, eleven-twenty)*
Man's made up.
Red. Roe. Ver.

One man decides he can't cross a number
of years, love a woman
he loves
because she's *x*
years old, witness to a thousand
extra noons,

because time's decided
her belly will be hers alone, no room
for a kid.

Forget the sun's
beautiful positions, how it raised
freckles he slowly licked.
Her body of hidden eggs
dropped baskets
she didn't know
she held.

Her breasts will be
just breasts.

Along highways,
wooden white crosses
mark slits in seconds
where some body's soul
crossed the line
between life and
x, slipped away
like   *that.*

Red. Roe. Ver.
Kids call a girl's name.
Bare-branch legs
drive her
to the line of arms
waiting for
her flat chest.

It's a game.

She might break through.

DEAR ANNETTE,

you are ten years into
your new dead life.
our mother is losing
her words.
which makes her kinder.
newer. annoying
in a simpler way.
now my head slips to how
she'd like to say
the simple, kind thing
we wanted: *dear.*
beautiful. mine.

but simply can't.
her tongue stuck
on *thing.* on *what-*
do-you-call-it.
those unmouthed sounds
I know now
are what made you,
dear sister,
silent as the ashtray
soaking up heat.
your reddening
nose. kleenex in the hand
you held near
eyes that wouldn't look
at me sitting
in the stiff-backed chair
of our youth.

words make actions.
actions lead to words.
my brain
couldn't hear

get up. go hold
your only sister.
that silence
was the nothing. the anger
that made me want to hit
your three-year-old daughter
for not knowing
how to tie her small pink shoes.

medicine makes our mother's voice
lilt into what I could call
sweetness. still

what she says
is nothing.
(it took me an hour to clean the back room.)
and nothing.
(why do you wear your hair like that?)
terrible is the word
she never forgets.

in your new dead life,
are there mothers?

your daughter
has your thick eyebrows
and small fisted
breasts. she gets angry.
over the phone
I blow kisses. send wishes.
we say, *I love you. I love you.*
I love you more. ten years
into your new dead life.
we carry phones.
can you give us a call?

GHOST

There is a ghost in this room,
a woman with breath like
a heavy party dress. She

is over in the corner, sitting on
the hard wooden chair, legs spread,
elbows on thighs, body hunched

like a man who is doomed because
he's done wrong or because circumstance
is painting his sad portrait.

She breathes like a cat. I know that,
really, there is a cat in the corner of the room
I sleep in, a cat that killed a mole,

delivered it to my doorstep, small and sleepy
and licked wet. I was at a party.
A man came up to me, said, *I just saw a ghost,*

but what he meant was an old lover,
someone who had left the days of his life
like they were chicken bones and tinfoil

in a black-green bag on the back stoop,
a heap waiting to be lifted up, carried away.
Now I have these days and these nights of ghosts.

I don't mean to suggest that the one
in the corner, now, as I am not sleeping,
as the man I say I love heats my body effortlessly,

is that woman. It is more complicated than that.
Let me just say, again, that now I have these days
and these nights, let me just say I hear ghosts.

THE LAST VOICE

comes clearly
in the footsteps

of the one-legged man
who lives above me,

who uses 5 a.m.
as an application

for a new life,
one he fills out

in Morse code,
a life where two legs

feel the solidity
of sidewalks,

where the hardness of
the earth's layers—

rock and rock and rock—
offers comfort.

He'll never get it.
I take my two worn shoes,

throw them one at a time

at the ceiling, go back
to my dreamy dreams.

SHE DIED.

Percodan daughter   kiss

of dead hair

bedpan can   tight elastic

waistband

you let her

morphine hand

smoke in bed   breast

done in

as a last day

oh the tv

burn down this house

lips slack

as mashed potatoes

spoons of lies   they drip

and dry

all talk gone

finger-on

Chapstick   razor

her bone-burnt legs

breast done   nipple-

less   tv on

on on   prison sister

asks for her last

supper   chili

her own hand-

written

recipe she eats

a whole bowl.

That was

good

THE SKY IS RIGHT

I do not want to wake up.
It is still dark,
but a teacup
round and perfect and blue
floats in the black air
outside my window
like just another star,
just another strange blue moon
with a handle.

I don't want to start living again,
I say, knowing the teacup is a messenger.
I say, *Dead people are talking to me in my sleep.*
I have to believe they know more than I do
and more than you can tell me.

The cup doesn't talk back.
I open the window, grab onto the handle
thinking *warm sweetness in my sleepy mouth,*
thinking *my future in tea leaves at the bottom.*

I float straight up.
One star becomes a cigarette,
another an armchair.
I sit back and the sky tells me
that this is the past, and it is simple.
The sky is right.

All the people I've ever loved,
dead or alive,
are in fields across the country
playing baseball,
and no one wants anything
they cannot have.

DEAR HEART,

      before the girl nub
         the sucking thumb
            there you were

       off-kilter circle
          blood plumber
   comforter of knives

if you were a deer's
I'd eat you
       (Split in half, remove vents and ducts)
hear with your straight-up ears

if you were a yolk
I'd stab and spill you

       (Leak dead voices, find forsaken keys)

      the start of your beating
  was my end

         wet tomato seed
      cooked pinto bean

(Rinse in water to remove all blood. Dredge in flour. Fry in butter.)

      will you marry me

     gray-blue stump
  brain of my brain
       soul's tongue
you came first   proved I was

    you come last

             then come again

HEAVEN, AS WE KNOW IT

My dead sister and I
are walking down the street.
She is here because
I am lonely and she understands
and because
this woman with the most beautiful breasts
just walked by,
and no one else,
not even this friend
who hasn't died yet
and who is walking with us,
can understand what I mean
when I say,
Her breasts are so beautiful.
I wish this street
were the desert in winter at sunset
and we were lying down
talking about the most perfect foods
we have ever eaten,
and that is simply all.

I love these beautiful things.
I love putting words together.
And I love all this listening,
which isn't just in my head,
which is heaven.

NOTES

The quote in "Night Eats the Last of It" is from Annie Proulx's *The Shipping News*.
"What Might Be Galaxies at My Feet" is inspired by Galway Kinnell's "Daybreak."
"It's a Good Day" is for JY.
"Dear Panties" is for Aaron Smith.

ACKNOWLEDGMENTS

Grateful acknowledgment is given to the following journals, in which poems originally appeared, sometimes in slightly different form:
5 AM, Mid-American Review, Prairie Schooner, River Styx, Threepenny Review, West Branch, and *Southern Poetry Review.*

Thanks to the Jentel Foundation, the Kimmel Harding Nelson Center for the Arts, the Pennsylvania Council on the Arts, and the Pittsburgh Foundation for their generous support. Thanks—from the heart of me—to my family and friends, especially Jan Beatty, John Fleenor, Sherrie Flick, Dani Leone, and Kristin Naca for their guidance, writing and otherwise. Extra thanks to dear Aaron Smith and dear Lois Williams. Thanks to my teachers. Thanks to Gerald Stern for seeing and hearing this. And thanks, thanks to Tom Kizer for the present and future.